I Already Have It All!

The God-Given Creative Power In Your Hands!

Brian Anderson-Payne

DEDICATION

I dedicate this book to the many souls that are waking up
daily. You're taking the experiences life is handing you
and you're turning them into fuel. God's greatest
blessings to you on your journey.

ACKNOWLEDGMENTS

For someone who accidentally became an author on purpose, I've truly come to appreciate the book birthing process. While it's possible to do it alone, I appreciate having a team that always works diligently to help give life to something that will give life to others.

Book Cover: NCA Designs
Editor: Bethany Sledge
Proof Reader: Ruby Anderson-Payne
Page Layout: Gwendolyn McCalep
Marketing Consultation: Wayne Taft Harris, Jr., Vanessa Collins

"Brian's book is a mixed bag of wisdom salted with scripture that should be consumed slowly."

- Victor Antonio
Television Host of Life Or Debt

Brian Anderson Payne's perspectives on Life, Purpose, Goal-Setting, and Achieving Your Dreams are incredibly profound. As a Life Strategist myself, I share similar views on Passion and I am thrilled to see Payne's simple, yet profound and relevant revelations articulated in a manner where the reader cannot help but understand and comprehend. It is an "easy, yet powerful read" that gets to the point of the matter. Believe me, YOU won't go wrong having this Powerful Life Tool in your possession or library!

-Undrai F. Fizer
Author of "The Excuse-less Life; 34 Inner-laws for Living Above Distraction"

Table of Contents

Forward

Having written a devotional book based on the 23rd Psalm myself some years ago, I am very keenly aware of how much more there is to say about the beautifully, simple yet profound poetry of David's timeless masterpiece. In 'I Already Have It All', Brian Anderson-Payne holds up this diamond to the light, turning it in such a way that new facets of revelation are captured and revealed in brilliant bursts of God-colors. The title of the book alone is an affirmation that everyone of us should be reminded of daily, because just like the characters in the Wizard of Oz, we generally don't realize what we already have inside of us until someone holds up a mirror of truth and shows us our own awesome reflection. This is a universal truth that every individual must learn to embrace in his or her own life. I have joyfully watched Brian's progression over the years, and believe that it's obvious to anyone who is connected with him that his own personal growth and evolution are reflected in his enlightened writing.

He is an out-of-the box communicator whose fearless transparency and perceptive insights are guaranteed to bring out the best in his readers. Be prepared to re-think what you already know as you immerse yourself in the pages of this very "next-level" volume!

Bishop Jim Swilley
*Founder, Metron Community; Bishop of Now Mini*stries

1

I ALREADY HAVE IT ALL!

The Lord Is My Shepherd. I Have Everything I Need. Psalm 23:1

The confession: *"The Creator of all things, whom I call God, is personally concerned about me and is actively involved in my life. Through His meticulous creation of all things, including me, He displays a genuine and daily concern for my life and my well-being. Therefore, I have confidence that my every need is now and always has been already met in Him, and he/she/it is found inside me."*

The quintessentially powerful nugget: We already have every necessity to obtain the life we desire. It's a simple truth, but grasping it may take a little digging. Fortunately, the digging has already been done. The facts: All our needs have been met. The work is just realizing and accepting it.

One man says, "My needs are not met! I don't have food to eat." I challenge his belief. Is there no food anywhere in the world? What would Kroger, Walmart or even the nearest corner gas station say about that? The good news is food is available. The bad news is it isn't in *his* refrigerator. First, just relax in the fact that there *is* food. The next step might be formulating the plan to get it from one location to another, but let's embrace the good. There *is* food to eat. The obstacle isn't the existence of food. The obstacle is getting it where you want it to be. There are quite a few ways to make that happen. Some are acceptable while others aren't, but the foundational point I'm making, and I hope you get it, is that food is available.

A woman says, "I don't have peace. My family is shattered, my finances are lacking, things are out of order, and because of this, I have no peace." She prays for peace and says she can't or won't have peace because she's waiting on God to provide it. In truth, peace (or the route to it) already exists. Now the responsibility, though imaginably difficult to achieve, lies in her ability to make choices to move her life in the direction of the thing she desires. Doing so could require therapy, self-reflection, awareness, counseling, a job change, divorce or separation from a marriage that no longer serves her, or a host of other choices. Nonetheless, the existence of peace is indisputable.

Every day, we cross paths with people with a myriad of experiences. One is utterly filled with joy while another miserably experiences the day. The difference between the two and what they have or haven't obtained isn't a result of intelligence, resources, family background or any other external feature. The difference lies in the understandably challenging decision to move in the right direction. The fact is still true. Joy does undeniably exist. It is one of those areas that stands available to all who are willing to pursue it.

Here is an important view. I lack nothing. Any other view suggests that what you desire is out of your reach. In that case, someone other than you holds the key to your happiness. This is more than just a confession. It's a vital point of perspective.

Daily, parents tell children, "You can accomplish anything you put your mind to!" As children, we accept this statement. As we grow and experience disappointments, failures and losses, it can become work to avoid the conclusion that some things just aren't for us. The majority of mankind has settled for the mundane reality of mediocrity. Disappointing experiences and painful losses work to train us not to reach too high for fear of the possibility of having yet another loss.

If we lose a second-grade relay race and then a third-grade relay race, and perhaps a fourth-grade race, we're courted by the idea that there are others who are simply faster than we are. Certainly, there are those who just have more natural ability than we have. While that's true, more importantly, those losses often hide the fact that we are capable of accomplishing much more than we typically do. We are capable of becoming a better, faster, more skillful runner. Michael Jordan is, arguably, the greatest basketball player ever. However, he didn't begin his career holding that title. Will Smith is one of Hollywood's most bankable actors. He could probably play any role because he's just that good of an actor, but his career didn't begin that way. He admits to struggling to watch his earlier roles. While the idea that *doing better is just a choice to do so* may sound basic and elementary, it's pretty accurate. Picture a personal goal you have and ask this question. *How bad do I want it?*

HOW BAD DO YOU WANT IT?

What prevents so many of us from obtaining our goal isn't our inability to do so but our unwillingness to maximize our full potential.

"Do what others won't do so you can have what others won't have."

Some of our most beloved heroes and the unimaginable victories they've accomplished demonstrate that winning isn't the result of a magical incantation. They show us that it's the byproduct of that immeasurable spirit given to man. If you want it, determine that you want it and work toward it. Move away from magic ideas and time-wasting distraction of waiting on a lucky break. Accept the belief that we are the masters of our destiny, and sculpt your mind and body into a force that simply won't be denied.

We are far more powerful than we are cognizant of. This is documented, factual information. How encouraging it is to discover things you're already capable of and you simply weren't aware of! What an amazing boost to our spirits to discover our ability to defy the odds in the many ways that we already do so on such a regular basis. Take a look at these amazing, godly bodies we possess. They are, to put it simply, works of art. Here are just a few facts you may or may not be aware of, but they will no doubt remind you of your greatness.

- Your brain's memory has the potential capacity to hold 2.5 million GB of data. That's roughly three hundred years of video.

- A newborn baby, pound for pound, is actually stronger than an ox.

- Your nose can remember about 50,000 different smells.

- If the human eye were a digital camera, it would have a resolution of 576 megapixels.

- The liver has an incredible ability to regenerate itself. Because of this, you can donate up to 50 percent of your liver for transplant and it will regenerate itself.

- The human body is estimated to have 60,000 miles of blood vessels. (The circumference of earth is 25,000 miles.)

- Our eyes can distinguish up to ten million color surfaces and take in more information than the largest telescope known to man.

- Our lungs inhale over two million liters of air every day. Their surface area is large enough to cover one side of a tennis court.

- In one square inch of our hand we have nine feet of blood vessels, 600 pain sensors, 9000 nerve endings, 36 heat sensors and 75 pressure sensors.

- Read more: Interesting Facts about the Human Body / Amazing Medical Facts of the Body | Medindia http://www.medindia.net/facts/index.asp#ixzz42FQQ26Jh

- Read more: Interesting Facts about the Human Body / Amazing Medical Facts of the Body | Medindia http://www.medindia.net/facts/index.asp#ixzz42FQDr3D9

- Read more: Interesting Facts about the Human Body / Amazing Medical Facts of the Body | Medindia http://www.medindia.net/facts/index.asp#ixzz42FPzqLVt http://www.cracked.com/photoplasty_1354_28-shocking-statistics-that-prove-human-body-magic/

I could keep this going for hours, but I'm sure you get the point. You are an amazing creation.

WE NEED TO BE BRAINWASHED

Changing the way we see the world and, more directly, the way we see ourselves is no easy task. It's arduous. Don't follow the trend to take the easy route. Raise the expectation you have of yourself. Lowering our expectations won't protect us from pain. In truth, lowering expectations beneath our potential, over time, actually increases pain. Depression is a result of a life half lived. Depression itself is the clear indication that we are internally convinced that there is more to life than what we are presently experiencing. The person who hates going to his job hates it because he realizes he's capable of so much more. The current job isn't filling a particular hole inside.

These negative emotions often signal that something about our paths needs to change. We have two options. Accept the pain, embrace it and determine that the good life simply isn't meant for us, or start the journey toward what fulfills us. It is simply not enough to pray and ask God to provide peace. That just isn't how any of this works. God doesn't give houses. Well, He could! Instead, He gives us trees. The finished product or house is the result of our choice to act with those trees.

Through the years, countless prayers have been prayed for an end to racism, sexism, ageism and the many other ism's. Indeed, God has answered. But horrible acts still occur. The reason is not because God wants them around. Clearly, we do. Surely, prayers for an end to segregation were prayed before the *Brown vs Board of Education* case in 1954. That's not the period when God finally got fed up with the whole racism thing. That's when man did! Likewise, God is not waiting on a specific date to eradicate the pressures and problems of your life. Perhaps, you are. God is your shepherd, and you have everything you need.

2

Positions
& Conditions

**He lets me rest in green pastures. He leads me
to calm water. Psalm 23:2**

We're discussing rest early in the conversation, yet we're not discussing things to rest *from* but *for*. With so much for us to accomplish, we prepare our minds, hearts and spirits early. Prepping early helps for a more successful outcome. Luke 14:28 in the Berean Study Bible says, *"Which of you, wishing to build a tower, does not first sit down and count the cost to see if he has the resources to complete it?"* We can cover the cost, and we will.

The Good Shepherd inside you describes a place of rest as one of abundance and one properly supplied with the necessary beneficial ingredients for a productive journey.

REST REQUIRED

What position would you say your life is presently in? Is it moving forward or stationary in still waters? Is it on full speed ahead or on pause? Either way, it's important knowing when and why to temporarily unplug from it all. It's a fast-paced world with lots of opportunities to become frustrated, anxious, overwhelmed or worried. These temptations are *weapons formed against those of* us who are out to take over the world with our great ambition. We see many areas to tackle. We desire to build our self-esteem, increase our income, repair our relationships, develop our spirituality and the list goes on and on. With all of the go, go, go, therein lies the need to schedule moments of effective rest. The Good Shepherd shows there are proper ways to rest that don't stop productivity, while improper resting techniques just equate to a stop in all forward motion.

We live in an extremely fast-paced world that seems to be getting faster. In this technological world, we can easily witness just how fast it is. Almost instantly, things become outdated and obsolete. This goes deeper than our preferred choices of fashion, current popular styles of music or acceptable dietary choices. More than gadgets, toys, foods and entertainment, notice how quickly our newborn babies reach adulthood or even how quickly we continually mature. Our world moves fast.

While this truth won't matter much to a toddler, it sure gives pause to those of us who are older. We question how much time we have left to accomplish our goals and dreams. How soon after acquiring our dream job will someone from the following generation have it offered to them? The girl in her twenties enjoys a date here or there, while the woman approaching forty worries that time is passing her by. Time becomes her tormentor, and she feels she has less of it.

In spite of society's nonstop message that we must 'go, go, go' and 'do, do, do,' it's our responsibility to schedule those moments when we can simply step back and unplug from it all.

We accomplish what we can while we can, but losing track of our need to refocus and refuel can actually leave us accomplishing less than previously possible. For instance, consider hurriedly racing to your appointment when you're already pressed for time. The thought of taking five minutes to stop for gas is unwelcome. Now, consider not stopping for those five minutes, running out of gas and needing to call AAA to refuel your vehicle. This example hopefully makes it vividly clear which of those decisions ultimately cost you more time.

RESTING OR STOPPING

Resting is stopping and continuing at the same time. It's a temporary halt to activity for the purpose of beginning again refreshed, refueled and refocused. Some of the things you're working on are too important to quit. You can't quit them, but you must rest from them. If not, even though they're important to you, you can end up under serving it, doing more damage than good. Things like self-development and self-discovery can be hard work. Occasionally, pull the plug to avoid feeling overwhelmed and under qualified.

Genesis 1 speaks of God *resting* on the seventh day after creating all of creation. One definition of *rest* is *freedom from activity or labor.* Clearly, there were other things to do. There was a created world full of potential but completely underdeveloped. Yet all of the first-level necessities were created. Now, it was time to go to the next level of creation but not before a brief pause in activity. God didn't stop all activity like a worker punching off a clock. He shifted activity to another role.

MINDFULNESS / MEDITATION / PRAYER

How do you stop and keep going simultaneously? Our bodies show us the example. Every evening at bedtime, we rest. We close our eyes and lose consciousness. As far as we know, everything has stopped. But in reality, it hasn't. The lungs are still filtering air. The heart is still pumping blood. The brain is still an operating command center. The concentration of the work just shifts from one team to another team with a different set of responsibilities. We spend a third of our lives sleeping, but don't for a second consider that unproductive time. It's not only productive time but a necessary time. Avoid sleep too long, and your waking hours aren't nearly as productive. We can't sleep life away, so we develop the ability to receive the benefits of rest while awake. Current popular practices for this include mindfulness, meditation and prayer. Surveys have shown that just ten minutes a day produce incredible results.

Here, we're not formulating a future plan or strategizing. Here, we are simply observing, listening and taking notes. It's the still moment when you simply observe how your body is feeling, without judging anything good or bad. It's being mindful of how you currently feel without redirecting your thoughts into any particular direction. It's analyzing previous steps taken and what worked about them and what didn't. It could be simply thinking on things you've already considered, without measuring their difficulty or how to accomplish them.

I believe in the value in prayer. For me, prayer is not a time for my godly *gimme list*. It's a time of communication with God. It can no more be rushed than can a conversation with your spouse. It's not a part of your 'to do' list, and treating it as such won't produce desired results. It's a time of talking and listening

22

without strings. You stop and you consider. This will perhaps be challenging to westerners because our culture is so 'motion driven.' It's difficult to willfully stop everything to just sit, reflect and listen. But you have to consider it just like your evening rest. Go too long without it, and the poor results show up in your ability to be productive. In ancient Israel, they had what was called 'solemn assemblies.' These were extended periods of time when entire bodies were called together to sit in silence, pray, repent and hear.

DIFFERENT STROKES, DIFFERENT FOLKS

Because there are *different strokes for different folks,* I decided not to list things that are considered restful. You know what works best for you. You know the things that bring you peaceful rest. Whatever those restful things are, they won't schedule time for themselves. You'll have to do that.

In the psalm, the location of rest for the sheep is described as green pastures. Picture a plush piece of land with delicious grass for sheep. It's not a brown, stale, desert land. The sheep will be able to eat their fill of nourishing ingredients. What are you currently eating on that's building you up for the task ahead?

EAT FOR THE ASSIGNMENT

If spiritual development is your goal, make sure you're pursuing the right kind of information to produce growth. If raising a productive child or grandchild in this generation is the goal, you may need to update the information you received from great-grandmother. Indeed, some principles are timeless, but practices may have greatly changed. A commitment to an outdated procedure or practice may be a loving act, but it could carry a disappointing outcome. Listening to brown, stale, outdated information won't work. Remember, you are what you eat.

How will you know if the information is healthy or stale? Is it producing the proper outcome? Pizza is great, but eating it for breakfast, lunch and dinner will soon show its inability to serve as productive nutrition. No one would have to tell you that. Just trying to be productive on such a diet will reveal its own inabilities. At that point, a new decision would have to be made. Discover something healthier and begin a new pursuit, or simply settle the weaknesses of the diet and level of productivity.

YOU KNOW WHAT'S BEST FOR YOU

It's such an elementary point to make that it almost seems beyond the need of being made. However, just noticing our chosen spiritual diets shows there is a need to emphasize it. Trying to become a more tolerant person is a difficult task on a diet of social media. Becoming a more accepting person proves difficult on a diet of horrific news events. While some may live on such a diet, it proves 'junk food' to me and my stated goals. I have to be able to tell myself, *That's not part of my diet,* and be able to trust my opinion even in light of other disagreeing opinions. While I may not yet know *all* that is good for me, I'm certainly aware of what's bad for me, and I have to trust my internal voice that says, "Avoid that." There's a lot of information to discourage you from trusting yourself. Social media bombard us with the opinions of others and their ideas of success. News media constantly remind us of what 'others' have to say about certain topics. There's enormous pressure for conformity. Even experts can be guilty of this. Certainly, we want to be advised and as well-informed as possible but not at the risk of silencing or distrusting that still, small voice inside each of us. Call it conscience, call it instinct or whatever you will. I call it God. The better we inform ourselves with good information, the better we are for it. But we have to balance our ever evolving intellect with our God-given ability to sometimes 'know what we know.'

MUTINY

Mutiny is when there's an open rebellion against the proper authorities, especially by soldiers or sailors against their officers. Mutiny is being attacked by your own team. We experience internal mutiny when our subconscious mind, which has been trained, fights against our current wishes. It looks like this: you want to move forward but your bad-thinking mind says, "You can't." You say you want to start a new direction, but your bad-thinking mind says it won't work. You've made up your mind. Today is the day to start the new workout plan, but mutiny happens and your bad-thinking mind says, "Nah, start tomorrow, and finish the bag of chips first." It's one thing to face opposition from others, but it's something altogether different when the opposition comes from within. One of the greatest obstacles to our inward guide is often other inward, more destructive tools that aren't always easily detectable. While many see their personal struggles as a result of a devil or the enemy, I'm more concerned about the 'inner me.' Within you, there's a battle that constantly attacks your desire to move forward. Truth is, there's no fight like the one you have on the inside, but you have to identify where the punches are coming from or it will be difficult protecting yourself.

"Float like a butterfly, sting like a bee. Your hands can't hit what your eyes can't see"
Muhammad Ali.

Destructive words coming from anyone outside us only have impact because of the supporting mutiny that happens inside us. Someone calling me a failure has absolutely no impact on me unless the 'inner me' has already suggested that such a statement is true. Every child has heard the phrase, "Sticks and stones may break my bones, but words will never hurt me." That's a very true statement unless the words that you tell yourself agree with the hurtful words you hear. In that case, words will devastate you, but it's not the words from without. It's the words that echo within.

"In our brains, there are two different systems for negative and positive stimuli. The amygdala uses approximately two-thirds of its neurons to detect negative experiences, and once the brain starts looking for bad news, it is stored into long-term memory quickly. Positive experiences have to be held in our awareness for more than twelve seconds in order for the transfer from short-term to long-term memory. Rick Hanson describes it in this way: "The brain is like Velcro for negative experiences but Teflon for positive ones."

https://www.psychologytoday.com/blog/wired-success/201406/are-we-hardwired-be-positive-or-negative

These can be alarming facts that I combat with Paul's words in **Romans 12:2 NLT**

Don't copy the behavior and customs of this world, but let God transform you into a new person by changing the way you think. Then you will learn to know God's will for you, which is good and pleasing and perfect.

STILL WATERS

Imagine the comfort of the sheep getting to drink from still waters. It probably wouldn't work trying to have the sheep drink from chaotic, rushing waves, so the shepherd finds still waters for them.

Today, it's important for us to be and find others who know how to still the waters. Working with teams on many projects, I really notice when a task is given to someone and he constantly acknowledges all of the difficulties in performing the task. I don't like being hammered with the problems. I like hearing solutions. I most enjoy working with people who come across difficulty and respond, "This is a problem, but there *is* a solution." These are people who defuse situations and don't ignite them. Believers are called to be peacemakers and problem solvers. Problem finders are a dime a dozen, but problem solvers are worth their weight in gold. In life's most chaotic seasons, search out still waters. You're designed to function in peaceful environments. That's why the Shepherd leads you to them. Help lead others to them by calming the waters.

YOU STILL GET TO CHOOSE

While I have absolutely no doubt that God keeps His end of the bargain by leading, guiding and nudging us in particular directions, the listening or following part of the deal is ours alone. It's still our responsibility to listen and follow. We're not robots. We still have the ultimate authority over the directions we take. If you want to take that money that seemed to show up miraculously just in time to cover that unexpected bill and buy a new pair of shoes instead of covering the bill, you're free to do so. But don't get upset when. . . .

SUMMARY

If the position (environment) you're presently in isn't set to a positive condition (atmosphere) aimed at productivity and progress, it's time to unplug (detach). While every environment doesn't exist to move you forward, guard the time you spend and the time you invest. Right now, you're after something, so invest the greatest time equipping yourself to possess those things. Take the classes. Watch the webinars, read the books. Find what feeds you best for the most productive journey, and eat.

3

Restoration And Right Directions

He gives me new strength. He guides me in the right paths, as he has promised. Psalm 23:3

Restoration: What is it?

Restoration is a nice, big, fancy word, but what is it? The definition is below.

> *: the act or process of returning something to its original condition by repairing it, cleaning it, etc.*

> *: the act of bringing back something that existed before*

> *: the act of returning something that was stolen or taken*

Simply put, restoration is putting something back in its original state. Obviously, restoration requires a great deal of insight. Total or perfect restoration won't work without knowing the original, perfect, intended state. We need the kind of sight that comes not from our eyes but from our God-given soul/spirit.

The restoration I'm speaking of here isn't some superficial level which simply deals with externals or 'band-aids.' I'm speaking of restoration at our deepest level, the restoration of our souls. The soul is the spiritual or the immaterial part of us. This requires much more than the bandage fixes we often use like money, materials or more possessions. Imagine: in a relationship badly damaged or even destroyed due to infidelity and loss of trust or simply growing in separate directions, finding a new relationship that brings joy isn't restoration. Moving from pain and hurt to anger or even aloofness isn't restoration. Building up a tough skin or lack of being impacted by the torn relationship isn't restoration. Training yourself not to 'feel' the hurt isn't what I'm speaking of either. Restoration, in this situation, would be delving into and understanding the causes of the breakdown and ultimately experiencing a progressive release of debilitating actions.

Real restoration doesn't happen without a clear picture of the original or intended state of being reached. We get that from God. Our increased conversation with Him or even self-reflection helps us discover our intended purpose for creation.

Without a picture of the original state, you can make something better than it currently finds itself but not truly restore it. Restore is to *store again*. Let's discuss a three-step process of eating, digesting and releasing.

EAT - DIGEST - RELEASE!

EAT

Why do we eat the particular foods we eat? It's simple. Because we want to! Unless you're force-fed, anything that goes into your body goes there because you put it there. There are many encouragers for the things we do, but the reason 'why' we do them is simple. We believed it would serve us in some way. After all, that's why we eat the foods we eat. After indigestion sets in about 2 in the morning, you're asking yourself why you ate whatever you ate. The answer is simple. You looked at it and thought, *That looks/smells really good, I want it, and I'm going to have it!* The painful results have you regretting your decision now, but remember that it was just that, your decision.

So it goes with life. Unless you had no choice in the matter, anything or anyone in your life is there because *you put it there.* Eating for me represents a conscious choice of consumption. With good or bad results, there's no need to deny what we've consumed. Come to grips with it. This is the spot where it's totally permissible and encouraged to identify the problems.

"Surgeons aren't afraid of a little blood!"

Denying or avoiding it won't work. In reality, denial never works. Yes, we made the wrong choice. Yes, we told the lie, or yes, we cheated, or yes, we weren't honest, or yes, we spent the bill money foolishly. Yes, we missed the opportunity. Yes, we took the wrong turn. This stage won't be extremely comfortable, but it's productive. This is the space where it's totally acceptable to tell our story. Admit every ugly little detail. Don't run from it or cower. Don't be afraid of it. Take your power back. It's our first step in serving it notice that its time of authority has come to an end. We can admit the issues here, even if only to ourselves, without fear. We're going under the knife of restoration, and surgeons aren't afraid of a little blood.

Don't spend time resenting your relationship when the truth is you invited it or allowed it. Maybe you didn't know the things you know now, but keep the responsibility in your hands. Don't waste time resenting the job that doesn't pay you what you're worth or appreciate your value. Acknowledge the fact that you filled out the application, took the interview and began the intake process. If the job no longer serves you, set a new course, but do so realizing that you're not a victim. You get to choose who and what stays in your life. Look around you. Tell me who or what is in your life that you haven't chose to allow? If your kids are pressing you beyond measure and you simply don't know how to fix their behavior issues, that's fine. There are routes to take to accomplish that, too. However, keep in the forefront of your mind that you chose to have kids. If that's too much to agree with, we can agree that at least you chose the act, and kids are a possible result of such, right? The point it, you are not a victim. You are in charge. Whenever you're in charge, you have the power to change it! Bon appetit.

DIGEST

The digestive system works through a process far too complex for me to understand. However, the simple explanation is it takes whatever we've consumed and turns it into energy for future service. Initially, it doesn't get a vote in what we consume. However, after making a few wrong decisions, we figure out what does and doesn't work for us and learn to avoid the latter. I don't know how it knows what it knows, but it knows how to break everything down and send it to the proper areas. The things that we can use, it uses. After everything beneficial has been extracted, the remains are discarded.

INDIGESTION

Typically the "eat, digest, release" process is simple. However, I've added one step for those occasions when things don't go as planned. Just like eating, occasionally, we've ingested something that doesn't agree with us. Enter indigestion. We took in the wrong food or took in something at the wrong time. The pain of indigestion serves as a great teacher that we've made a misstep. Something about our routine needs changing. We start asking, "What was it? When did we have it?" Don't do that again! It doesn't work for us.

RELEASE

A process every bit as awesome as the digestion process is the 'releasing process.' Not to be crude, but hey, let's face it. This is fascinating. Our bodies masterfully extract every beneficial piece of what we've consumed, sends it to its most beneficial area, and eliminates all leftovers. Like clockwork, it gets rid of everything that no longer serves us. What was yesterday's energy is tomorrow's waste. If the body holds on too long to what no longer serves it, holding on only creates more problems.

We only need to look inside ourselves to see how to handle our greatest problems. It is not only useless but dangerous to keep holding the things that no longer serve you. No matter how long you've been friends with someone, if that friendship has reached the place where it no longer serves you, you don't win an award of selflessness for holding on to it. Holding on to a marriage that you no longer serve and/or it no longer serves you out of a need for comfort or commitment eventually turns into a greater problem. Holding on to a dream that no longer brings you joy, just for the sake of not wanting to feel like a quitter, will not bring satisfaction but disappointment. Come to grips with the reality that it no longer brings energy but has become 'waste,' and release it.

I spent a number of years sharing the difficulty I had from being abandoned at birth by my parents. It affected my self-esteem and the perspective of my value. It impacted the way I handled all my relationships. I discovered myself to be quite clingy or rather distant for fear of being abandoned again. What happened to me was real. However, after continuing to grow into the person who I wanted to be (and I'm still at that process), I realized I was holding on and reliving a story that was no longer serving me. I don't need to share that story anymore. Yes, it's true that it happened. But the telling of that story no longer brought me energy. It no longer served me, so holding on to it was like holding onto doo-doo. Why would I want to do that? I didn't, so I stopped and changed the story.

GOD WANTS YOU RESTORED

Nature teaches us that restoration is a God-given right to all life, not just humankind.

Cut a tree down while leaving the roots intact. Catch a cold while leaving the immune system intact. You'll find that restoration of your health isn't something you'll have to pursue. It's something that takes place automatically. Your body instinctively knows what to do to right the wrongs done to it. The prescriptions that doctors provide don't bring healing. They assist healing. Your body knows how to fight the viruses. It generally takes about three to five days, and tah-dah!

God's will for us is to live in a restored state. You don't have to ask or pray for it (though that *never* hurts) or even look for it. I'm certainly not suggesting avoiding doctors. I believe doctors are gifts to us that, many times, give us information that, properly followed, speed up our bodies' natural processes.

GET OUT OF THE WAY

Even though restoration is our gift, we want to assist it by simply getting out of the way. If your body has a cold, though you may not know the process taking place inside to right the wrong, you can assist the process by resting and choosing not to prepare for a marathon. Don't overwork your brain with other activities while it's helping you.

If a friendship has come to an end, don't invest time concentrating on what you could have done differently or even what you should do now to fix it. If you've set out to restore your self-esteem, don't invest time holding on to and rehearsing your flaws. You know they're there. You've accepted that. Now, get out of the way of restoration and take a new path. If it's necessary to avoid old environments that constantly remind you of your flaws, do that. There's no need for feeling guilty for desiring to advance yourself. Making yourself attend the family reunion where everyone loves to talk about that stupid thing you did thirteen years ago is a waste of energy. You're not committing to cutting off your family. You will show up again. You're just choosing not to do so at this time because it's slowing your restoration. When the process is complete and you're no longer terribly affected by the jokes and laughter, show up, if you so choose to. But until then, you're not doing yourself any favors and actually might be causing (or allowing) a bit of harm.

CALL TO ACTION:

- Release others from the expectation of understanding your battle. You're fighting a fight that others may know nothing about.

- Restoration isn't something we simply pray for and leave alone. You can't restore what you won't touch. Decide to prepare for surgery.

The pattern of the prodigal is: rebellion, ruin, repentance, reconciliation, restoration.

Edwin Louis Cole

Read more at:
http://www.brainyquote.com/quotes/keywords/restoratio n.html

4

Dungeons
and Dragons

*Even if I walk through a very dark valley, I will
not be afraid, because you are with me. Your
rod and your shepherd's staff comfort me.*
Psalm 23:4

Have you ever been in places and you can't figure
out how you arrived there because you would
never have chosen to be in such places? To
someone who grew up in the church environment I grew
up in, it's strangely encouraging to see David admit to
being in the 'valley of the shadows of death.' Oftentimes
in environments of faith, it's difficult to admit that things
are sometimes less than perfect. I think we sometimes
take on the unnecessary pressure of feeling like we have
to make God look good and thereby pretend that
everything in life is always wonderful. That's another
reason why I've developed an appreciation for
scripture's ability to often keep things in perspective for
me. Scripture doesn't hide the ugly truths that sometimes
arise.

Honestly, sometimes life just isn't what you dreamed it
would be. Sometimes, you're not where you thought you
would be when you thought you would be there. That's
not being negative. It's just stating the facts. Sometimes,

you're facing disappointments you never dreamed you would have to face. Sometimes, you're standing at the grave site of a loved one, wondering where you're going to get the strength to get through tomorrow. Sometimes, you're trying to figure out how in the world you're going to make ends meet when all the money you have is presently in your pocket, and it's clearly not enough. Sometimes, you just don't expect to be in positions where you find yourself. To say so is no indictment against God or your faith. It's just life.

DON'T GLAMORIZE THE GHOULS

In this positive-confession era, many say, "I have nothing bad in my world to face." Okay, that's fine. I don't personally subscribe to the idea of glamorizing ghouls myself, but positive confessions won't make that foreclosure notice disappear. Things have to be faced and admitted before they can be overcome, escaped or handled. After all, you can have the most up-to-date navigation system in the world. It can take you any place known to man, but in order for it to do its job, it has to be able to identify where you are presently.

Here in the verse, David said, "Yes, I accept that I'm walking through this valley of the shadow of death." Some things are what they are whether we admit or accept them or not. We can accept the fact that there will sometimes be dark places in life that we must tunnel through. However, we also accept the fact that we can always be successful on such journeys because we have and thereby become great traveling companions.

Each of us has his own dungeons and each of us has her own antagonists that we consider dragons. It's unnecessary to attempt to define or describe what they are because they're different for each of us. While writing, I'm using mine to describe scenarios, but you simply remove me and insert yourself wherever you fit.

Thanks to Hollywood, anytime I think of dungeons, my mind goes classical antiquity when soldiers strapped themselves with swords and shields. Imagine those places where you feel alone and under served.

Reflecting on my own dungeon-like scenario, I remember times feeling terribly alone even though I never truly was. Alone is exactly how you feel when you have to handle things without support or encouragement. However, you have to do it. No one can do it for you, no matter how much he may desire to. When you're ready to graduate to your next level, *you* have to take that last exam. You have to prove that you learned all the information necessary to equip you for the next grade.

I remember a situation where I unintentionally offended a few family members. Being the non-confrontational person that I've been, avoiding tense situations at all costs seemed a good plan. My past methods for handling conflict were to turn into an ostrich, stick my head in the sand and wait for the conflict to disappear. However, moving toward the person I wanted to be (which I'm still working on) demanded that I take the test and complete the class. God provides opportunities to show us if change is truly our desire. Even when we don't know who we truly want to be or how to get there, just making a decision is sometimes the all-important initial step. The universe will always provide you with what you need to get where you want or need to go.

My dungeon was the place of making a decision and

deciding to do what needed to be done. I had to pick up the phone and say, "I'm sorry," with no excuses or expectations attached. When you *grow*, you've got to *go*. What makes it feel like a dungeon is the feeling of aloneness because no one is going to do the work for you. There are things you're going to have to handle yourself. You will sometimes feel alone in what you have to do. Even if you're married or your home is constantly full of people, even if you're always surrounded by people, there will be places where you feel you're totally alone. Don't focus on the difficult side of it. See the fact that God thinks enough of you to take opportunities to deal with you in solitude. There are places where God wants to deal with you outside of all other distractions.

JACOB'S DUNGEON

Genesis 32:22-32 records the epic battle between Jacob and God. It's the battle Jacob traveled through his dungeon of self-discovery. He had to face the consequences of yesterday; he had to embrace the fact that he hadn't been the person he wanted to be. That moment allowed him to decide who he wished to become. Everyone spends moments in the dungeons to determine who he is truly going to be. You don't have to come up with an answer. Just listen.

According to Matthew 26:36, even Jesus, with all the power, clarity, purpose and vision that He had, spent time in the dungeon alone. Even if you take people with you, they won't always feel like they're with you. Jesus criticized His companions briefly but then quickly let go of it. Why? He fully understood that each of us must have those moments of destiny. You can pull on the encouragement you receive from others, but the decision to fight or flee will be yours and yours alone.

How will you handle the dark moments of your past? How will you handle the disappointments others handed you? How will you handle resentment in light of your new awareness that moving forward requires letting go of the past? How you say you'll handle it is fine. However, the situations will eventually present themselves and you'll get to decide truly how you will handle them.

In Hollywood, dragons are as menacing as their creators dream them to be. Some have multiple heads and tower many feet in the air. Some breathe fire and emit the most terrifying sounds. It's always up to the imagination of the creator. The dragons all look different, based on imagination. Jesus' dragon was death. Jacob's dragon was his brother Esau. David's dragon was King Saul. My dragon was abandonment. Only you know what your dragon is. However, what it is or was isn't nearly as important as who you are and who's with you!

GOD IS ALWAYS THERE

It's comforting to know that whatever situations we find ourselves in and however we got there, God is still with us. Some believe that God is unquestionably there in situations they believe He orchestrated but not in those situations that result from their decisions of deliberate disobedience. They think He somehow just stands still and waits on them to get themselves together. Nothing could be further from the truth. Even thinking so gives validation of their actions to treat their loved ones in the same manner. The father who believes God treats us this way feels validated when he shuts the door on his teenage daughter for getting pregnant. God is always with you. In truth, in those most disappointing places of our lives we truly witness the limitless love of God. Real love doesn't take breaks. In struggles, even of our own making, love doesn't slack off but actually kicks into high gear.

Where can I go to get away from your Spirit? Where can I run from you? If I go up to the heavens, you are there. If I lie down in the grave, you are there. Psalm 139:7-8

Sometimes, you find yourself wondering if God is really with you or if He's left you. The next time you question if the presence of God has left you, try this. Check to see if your heart's still beating twenty-four hours a day nonstop, even while you sleep. Check to see if your red blood cells are still carrying oxygen throughout your body or if your white blood cells are still fighting off infectious diseases that you weren't even aware of. If your lungs are still getting rid of carbon dioxide and exchanging it for oxygen, then that means there's something so magnificent going on in your body that even you can't explain how or why it's happening. I'm pretty sure that God is still with you.

However, even with the constant presence of God on your side, there will still be ugly situations you encounter or even create. God chaser or not, there's no avoiding this. Life is life. The comforting part is He will be with you; therefore, you will be with others.

He is always with you, and that's pretty noteworthy, seeing that there are times we don't always seem to be with ourselves. Sometimes, we seem to just check out.

Periods of overwhelming depression or guilt make us question if we're truly 'with ourselves.' We speak bad of ourselves or our thoughts are utterly negative and self-condemning. God doesn't do that to us. Even the Godlike portion of ourselves never do that. Your body is always working for you and never against you. It doesn't work to tear you down. Even if an external virus enters and gives you a cold or anything else, your body always works to 'right the wrong.' I remember going on a ski trip once where I sprained my ankle. Even though the trip was my decision, my body still went to work on fixing the problem. My body didn't say, "Oh, well, you shouldn't have made a decision to do something that could bring us harm." No, it always works for us. That's how God is. No matter where you go or how you got there, God goes right along with you.

Yes, I'm in a Bad Place, but I Have Great Company. Companionship Trumps Conflicts!

No need to deny the dungeons of life. It won't make them go away. More so, the need to want to deny them becomes less once you've embraced the truth that your Companion enables you to conquer them. As a child remember how less scary the monster under the bed became once Mom or Dad entered the room? You didn't concern yourself whether the monster was there or not. It didn't matter. Who cares who's under the bed as long as Dad is sitting on the bed with you?

'But' has become one of my favorite words in the English language. I didn't have this appreciation for the word in grade school, but now that I understand it, I love it. 'But' is a negative conjunction. It changes the direction of the sentence and cancels everything said before it. If your boss says, "I really wanted to give you the promotion, but . . . ," do you honestly care about the first part? You only want to know what follows the 'but.' I often jokingly say, "Just start at the 'but' part!" Indeed, you may be in a difficult section of life now, *but* the all-knowing, all-powerful God of the universe is with you. So who cares about the hurdles? You can jump them.

POSITIVE PROCLAMATIONS OR LIES

(I Samuel 21:12, II Samuel 6:9, I Samuel 21:10, 20:1, 19:18)

I have a unique way of looking at things. We all do if we don't allow the pressure of public opinion to dumb us down. I read David's words that he feared no evil because God was with him and immediately thought, *Wait a minute, David. Yes, you did fear evil! You feared evil several times in life. You might not have been afraid of the lion or the bear you faced in I Samuel 17, but you were certainly afraid of Saul in I Samuel 21. You may not have been afraid of the terrifying giant, Goliath, but you sure were afraid of King Achish. Yes, David, there were times when you definitely were afraid!*

Was David lying to us? Was he purposely attempting to deceive us? I don't believe so. I think he was simply obeying the lyrics of the song, "Give Thanks," which says, "And now let the weak say I am strong; let the poor say I am rich because of what the Lord has done for us. Give thanks."

It's not that David wasn't afraid. However, sometimes just knowing who is in your corner can stir your courage and confidence. We'll discuss that more soon.

I'd like to consider that David wasn't lying but rather giving a prophetic proclamation. What's the difference, you ask? You may consider it semantics, but I see it much deeper than that. By definition, a lie is: a false statement made with deliberate intent to deceive; an intentional untruth; a falsehood.

People lie for protection from current realities. You give positive proclamations to change your current realities. You're ten minutes late to work and the boss is on the warpath. He's the first one you see after entering the door. The first question is: "Why are you late?" Instead of being honest and running the risk of reprimand, you lie and say you had a flat-tire. The purpose of the lie was to protect yourself from the possibility of being reprimanded in your current reality. However, if you enter the same doors daily and repeat to yourself, "I own my own company and I'm my own boss. I am successful, supplied and effective," some would say that's a lie because it's not your current reality. However, others of us would say it is a current reality that you've envisioned and now begun the process of manifesting that which you see in your mind. This eventually changes your action steps, thereby ultimately changing your reality. In other words, lies are fear based. Prophetic proclamations are faith based and lead you into a new direction.

PUBLIC PRESENTATIONS WITH PRIVATE RESERVATIONS

Honestly, sometimes we're afraid. Sometimes, David was afraid. However, you would not always know that because of his ability to shake off fear and do what needed to be done. Sometimes, we're looking at others and the confidence they display, and conclude: "I could never have that much confidence!" First, stop the comparisons. I'm sure that some looked at David during those times of great triumph and concluded this guy must be the most confident person on the earth. Because of his victories, some may have never concluded that David was ever afraid. Actually, if I couldn't read his thoughts, I would have struggled to believe it myself. Thankfully, Scripture records the story so we can see it clearly. .

One popular acronym for fear is: *False Evidence Appearing Real.*

The dictionary.com definition says:

> **Fear:** *A distressing emotion aroused by impending danger, evil, pain, etc., whether the threat is real or imagined; the feeling or condition of being afraid.*

I list the popular acronym because, for the most part, fear is not real. It only appears real. It doesn't really exist. It doesn't possess matter. It's not an actual thing. It's in your mind, and therefore only gets to be as real as we allow or cause it to be.

Clinical brain neurologist Dr. Mark Waldman teaches that 90 percent of your worries, fears and doubts are just memories from the past projected onto your future that aren't real. In other words, we typically fear things that aren't real or have never really happened. We could have had something happen in the past, and fear takes the memory of that situation and projects it onto our future and creates emotions about a situation we haven't even experienced. It's not real. Take little children, for instance. I've seen several children, including my own, experience a stage when they are afraid of the bogeyman. They sometimes have great fear concerning this foggy character. Here's the thing. They've never really seen this menacing image they're so afraid of. We know they haven't because it doesn't exist. No doubt, they may have had a negative experience in the past, but the imagination then takes the experience and creatively constructs something we call the boogeyman. However, in truth, he's not real. He's something we created.

I think of the many times I've played scenarios over and over again in my head, concerning the possibility of how something could go wrong. Many times in the past, I found myself afraid to have certain conversations because of how I believed they could have gone awry. Did you hear that? I was afraid of doing something real because of something fake. Many have felt that. That's one of the reasons people don't follow their dreams. It's not that they're not capable of fulfilling them. They are capable. It's just that they're often too afraid to try because the fear of how it *could* turn out keeps them paralyzed.

Many avoid relationships because of a past heartbreak, and the memory of the past keeps projecting itself onto their future. Just the fear of yesterday hinders them from enjoying today and robs them of the possibility of having a tomorrow. Don't let this happen. Check your fears. The majority of them aren't real, and those that remain aren't able to stop you, should you decide not to be stopped.

GOD DIDN'T CREATE A WORLD OF FEAR FOR YOU

If you're living in a world of fear, recognize and admit that it's not God's will for you. Accept that. Then change it.

II Timothy 1:7 says it this way:

For God has not given us a spirit of fear and timidity, but of power, love, and self-discipline.

Fear isn't our birthright. That's why God didn't give it to us. You have to go find it for yourself. If God gave it to us, we'd have it at birth. Babies aren't afraid of heights. They'll roll right off the bed if you let them. They're not afraid of ferocious dogs or even snakes or lions. No, fear isn't our birthright. We have to move away from the confidence that God gives us to learn fear. Life is no slacker in presenting us with situations to rob us of that birthright of courage. Many of the hurtful, harmful situations we experience as children are the conduit for introducing us to that fear. One or two situations can happen, and once the seed of fear has been planted, we often water it until God interrupts the process by causing a mind renewing to take place.

CREATE BY LIGHT

Interestingly, when I first began outlining this chapter, I spoke of a healthy benefit of a reasonable portion of fear. Psychologists discuss a beneficial level of fear which discourages bad decisions, like fear of going to jail keeps you from stealing, or fear of divorce keeps you from cheating, and so on. It's a popular theory often taught today. While I understand the theory, I'd like another alternative to creating by darkness instead of light.

In the beginning God created the sky and the earth. The earth was empty and had no form. Darkness covered the ocean, and God's Spirit was moving over the water. Then God said, "Let there be light," and there was light.
Genesis 1:1-3

According to Genesis 1:2, there was a time when darkness engulfed the earth. You know what happened next, right? God said, "Let there be light." He didn't say, "Oh, Me, what's all this darkness? I'm so tired of darkness. You know You must protect Your Spirit from darkness!" No, He didn't say any of those things. He just said, "Let there be light." His astoundingly simple but profound example shows us what to do with our 'dark' situations. Create by light. Our conversation should be about what we want, not what we don't want. It should be about the kind of people we want to attract into our lives, not about those we're trying to get away from. Let it be about the life we want, not the one we're tired of. His example says create by light. Therefore, it's not that we don't have fears. We just focus more on what we want than what we don't want. We then follow David's step, we continue to confess we fear no evil because "the good" or God is with me!

In the psalm, David said he found comfort in the shepherd's rod and staff. Typically, during that time, shepherds would always have a rod with them. Mostly, they were for protection against predators. The staff, perhaps more than any other tool, identified the role of a shepherd. The staffs were typically designed with the particular shepherd in mind. It fit his height, his size and his strength, as larger shepherds may have larger staffs. While the rod may have been used mostly for protection of the sheep, the staff was typically used *on* the sheep. It was used to correct them, guide them or even scold them. What a picture! *Comforted by correction!*

COMFORTED BY CORRECTION

You can actually feel comfort in correction. I'm not one who personally believes that God punishes us for our bad choices. It doesn't fit with my psyche. I can't connect the idea that God punishes me *and* He allowed Jesus to take my punishment on Calvary's cross. I can't accept both of them. Even this world's judgment system believes in what is called double jeopardy. Double jeopardy: *a procedural defense that forbids a defendant from being tried again on the same (or similar) charges following a legitimate acquittal or conviction.*

Surely, society's system isn't more benevolent that God's system. However, I do believe that God allows the process of sowing and reaping to occur. If you sow the seed of cruelty to a relative by treating him unkindly, you could reap a harvest of his turning from you. If you sow a seed of adultery, you could reap a harvest of divorce. If you sow a seed of anger and foul language, you may reap a harvest of violence. If negative things return to you, that's not God's punishment. That's the result of you being a great farmer. Those returns can be great encouragers for making better choices to those of us who can be a bit hardheaded.

To know that God desires the very best for us and allows teachers to present themselves in a myriad of areas is comforting. It's not always enjoyable but comforting nonetheless. As we mature, we come to appreciate the people who thought enough of us to tell us "no" when they believed it would further our progress. We grow to appreciate the parents who told us we couldn't do what we wanted to do because of our previous bad decisions, though at the time, we thought them sworn enemies of life! Yes, many times, it's only in retrospect we value and find comfort in the 'rods and staffs' of life.

Brian Anderson-Payne

5

Selected to Show Off

*You prepare a banquet for me, where all my
enemies can see me; you welcome me as an
honored guest and fill my cup to the brim.*
Psalm 23:5

SHOWOFFS AND STANDOUTS

As a kid in grade school, I didn't really enjoy
when other kids had the opportunity show off. It
didn't matter if they were showing off a new toy
they just received or new clothes. Whatever it was, if
they were showing it off, I wasn't the happy camper.
Why did that bother me so? Now, more mature, I've
discovered the problem, and sadly, it was more my
problem than theirs. I was jealous. If I had received
something new, I would have no doubt been doing the
same thing, showing off. No matter how uninterested I
or any of the other jealous kids appeared to be, the
celebrants were not impacted. They didn't allow our
disinterest to hinder their celebration in the slightest
way. I'm not even sure if they noticed. They just kept
right on showing off.

What's wrong with showing off anyway? They weren't
putting the rest of us down for not having what they had.
They were just being excited about their new thing. They
had something new, and they were excited about it. Why
shouldn't they have been allowed to gloat for a bit? If
you have something you're delighted about, you should

53

be allowed to show it off. If you're glad to finally have a happy relationship after years of loneliness and aloneness, show off. If you're thrilled to have a car after countless bus rides and walks, show off. If you're blissful to have your own business after years of making millions for others, show off. Celebrating your win isn't declaring another's loss. Actually, if it brings you joy and it's not at the expense of others, it's okay for a little show off, even if the other jealous kids don't think so.

We're born with an incredible sense of ambition and drive. In our youth, we are limitless in our beliefs and potential. We believe that anything is possible. Ask any child what he wants to be or what she wants to do when they grow up, and prepare to see imagination at its best. They may express the desire to be wizards or animals or to fly around the world with wings, or all sorts of things. They will continue to believe in their dreams until dream killers come along to explain how and why they can't do or be what they desire to be someday.

ENVIRONMENT MATTERS

Your environment matters. Where you are and whom you're around impacts how you feel. When you're around positive people, you feel more positive. Around negative people, you feel more negative energy. That's the reason I support the idea of surrounding yourself with those who believe in your limitless possibilities. If we allow positivity to be stripped of its authority in our lives, sadness, pain, discomfort and other negative feelings are all that remain.

There comes a time when silence is betrayal.

- Martin Luther King Jr.

In the Psalms text, not only do I see the support that God showed David, but it's also notable *where* He showed that support. He showed His support of David right in the face of David's enemies. Private support has no public power. Your support has to stand up and be counted. You'll know when your public support is needed. And I don't recommend you expecting those times always to be comfortable or convenient.

The ultimate measure of a man is not where he stands in moments of comfort and convenience, but where he stands at times of challenge and controversy.

- Martin Luther King Jr.

WITH YOU WHEN YOU'RE RIGHT

I have an aunt, Joanne, who lives in Indianapolis. She's one of the hippest seniors I know. She turned seventy-one on her 2015 birthday. She can still get around better than most twenty-somethings, too. I remember one of her popular catch phrases when I was a kid. Anytime someone said anything she was in agreement with, you could hear her voice ring out with, "Now, I'm with you when you're right!" That was her way of saying, "I agree with you." I always think of Aunt Joanne when I hear those words. Yet today, when I hear those words, my mind asks another question. *What about when I'm wrong?* I've never heard a cliche speak about being with anyone when they're wrong. Having a chorus of supporters when you know you're clear of any wrongdoing is inspiring, but today, we're more prone to notice the faces of those who stand with us when we're wrong as two left shoes. I'm not speaking of consenting to our errors. I'm speaking of providing unwavering support in spite of them. After all, If I get caught robbing a bank, I wouldn't expect my loved ones to stand outside the jail and start a 'free BAP' campaign, but I don't think expecting an occasional 'I love you' letter or phone call is too much to ask.

SOCIETY PREFERS COMFORT
NOT COMMITMENT

Fact: Our society often prefers comfort over commitment. In the unfortunate revelations of infidelities and mishandling in the lives of well-known public figures, a wide range of emotions and public responses appear. Often, society is shocked when wives stay with self-control-lacking spouses with the ambitious hope of fixing what's been damaged. Peanut galleries all over the world ring out with their opinions. Some believe that staying in a marriage, a friendship or even a business partnership that has experienced betrayal is actually damaging. Those opinions say you have to respect yourself and get away from anyone who would break trust with you. I understand the view. But, as one who, shamefully, knows the power of a bad decision in areas of marriage, friendship and business, I know this view doesn't leave a lot of hope. There's a lot to be said about knowing you're loved by someone who chooses to see the best in you, even when you can't see it yourself. There's something powerful and restorative about a love that holds on to you without expectation of reciprocity.

GOD'S LOVE

It's difficult to comprehend a measure of God's love until you've been loved by someone who had every reason to give up on you but made a choice not to. God's love is so easy to place somewhere in the back of our minds because we read about it but often lack physical representations in front of us demonstrating the claims that Scripture makes about us. It's easy to hear or read Scripture and simply say, "Amen to that," but not really fathom the idea of someone actually loving us in such a capacity. While I think we hear far too few testimonies of individuals experiencing love like this, it's wonderfully encouraging knowing that such testimonies do exist! There are people working diligently and passionately to develop and share unconditional love. I'm purposely stressing this point to bring attention to it. The more we see it, the more we expect it. The more we expect it, the greater its platform becomes.

BEHIND ENEMY LINES

In the absence of light, darkness rules. Scientist have discovered that there's no such thing as darkness. There is only the absence of light. However, in the absence of light, darkness rules the day (pardon the pun). The slightest bit of light overrules the greatest amount of darkness. Just look up at the sky on the darkest night. You can see the stars even through the millions of miles of darkness separating us. The light still prevails.

Contrary to many opinions, the world isn't really getting worse. More light bearers simply need to reveal themselves. People are depressed not because their life is so bad. They're depressed because their eyes are closed to the enormous good surrounding them. People don't get divorced because they fall out of love. You can't fall out of something you never fell into. People get divorced because they can no longer see the things that initially brought them together. Situations don't have to change for feelings to change. Only perspectives do.

Some places don't provide the best perspective.

Hollywood has given me great pictures to work with concerning the idea of being behind enemy lines. It's typically always a bad situation for the character. The prisoners go through torture and other uncomfortable scenarios. It's not the kind of environment any of us would enjoy being in. I consider myself being behind enemy lines anytime I'm surrounded by those who refuse even to try to see the good in me. We don't want to be around people who can't see our greatest good. Yet we're often in such environments every day, and sometimes we don't even have to leave our houses. Many of us fight an enemy every day. The only enemy I choose to acknowledge is the 'inner me' enemy! Anything or anyone outside you can always be dealt with, if by no other means but simply escaping. You can always simply walk away from others or tune them out, but you can never get away from yourself. As the saying says, "Wherever I go, there I am."

How do you handle it when your own mind is the greatest obstacle? What do you do when you can't escape the one causing the problems? What do you do when the enemy is you?

NO SECRET CELEBRATIONS

In spite of all the people who love bragging on how unique they are (and by design, they really are), most people prefer to go along with the crowd. That's why we have trends or fads. Trends often stem from a number of people too fearful to step out as that uniquely original person God designed them to be. Rather than take the road less traveled, they simply follow the pattern already set. For some, it's frightening to be thought of as different. However, when you operate in your unique design, others can't help but notice the benefit you are because you're designed to be one. They identify the gift you are to their life. The fear of identifying with you may give them pause. They have to decide if identifying with you is worth risking their own acceptance and comfort (though anyone needing to consider this type of decision probably doesn't realize that he is already not being fully accepted). Their behavior resembles that of Nicodemus who came to admire and learn from Jesus in the middle of the night.

There was a Jewish leader named Nicodemus, who belonged to the party of the Pharisees. One night he went to Jesus and said to him, "Rabbi, we know that you are a teacher sent by God. No one could perform the miracles you are doing unless God were with him." Jesus answered, "I am telling you the truth: no one can see the Kingdom of God without being born again." John 3:1-3

Needing to feed from your table, but avoiding the cost of the meal. What do you do with such people who are willing to celebrate you in secret? You do just like Jesus did. You offer what you have been given because that's why you were born, but you don't make it more than what it is. Don't create any unrealistic expectations of your secret admirers. Do what you were created and intended to do, bless them how you can and keep it moving! In other words, those who aren't willing to celebrate or stand with you publicly don't receive the same investment of your time as those who do. You're here for a purpose. You have all the time you need to 'invest,' but you have very little to 'spend.'

> *Because of the miraculous signs Jesus did in Jerusalem at the Passover celebration, many began to trust in him. But Jesus didn't trust them, because he knew all about people. No one needed to tell him about human nature, for he knew what was in each person's heart.*
> *John 2: 23-25*

CHOSEN

David said God anointed his head with oil, and his capacity to receive was overwhelmed.

The word 'anointed' basically means *chosen* or *selected for a specific task*. Oh, the joy of being selected! Joy and pride come with knowing you've been chosen. There's a different feeling for the kid who's the first selection for the dodgeball team, versus the last kid who wasn't really *chosen* but simply selected for the team by default.

To be chosen in the midst of other options says that you've been preferred. If you have options and you make a choice, that choice emerges as your preference or the thing you prefer. If you had options, the job you took was preferred *over* others. I'm sure we all react to being preferred.

The things that makes adultery so devastating in the mind and heart of a spouse is its declaration that she, at least for some period of time, was no longer preferred. Adopted children sometimes require counseling for the sake of healing their thoughts that infer they were not preferred.

God choosing David, perhaps in front of his haters, undoubtedly built confidence. It allowed David to see that, over the desire of his enemies, he had been preferred.

THE OVERFLOWING CUP

It's wonderful to be preferred. Even better is being preferred *and* celebrated. Being preferred to be a wife for some is wonderful. Being a wife who is showered with love, joy, happiness, gifts, time, attention, loyalty, support and trust is even better. To the child waiting for adoption, to be chosen is wonderful. To be that child and be taken into a home where the one goal of that house is daily to make that child's every dream come true is even better. It's great to let people know that they are our preferred choice. Yet supporting that choice and backing it up with action are even better.

If you grow up in an environment where there's never enough of anything good, it can be challenging to outgrow the *just enough* mentality. I've experienced times where the money was so low that I just desired enough to get by! The concern wasn't wealth or plenty. The concern was simply having enough to pay the bills. You can notice when this mentality has been allowed to prevail in adults also. However, it's not God's desire for us to be stuck living this way.

El Shaddai
(THE MORE THAN ENOUGH GOD)

One of God's names is El Shaddai, which means 'more than enough' also God Almighty. God describes Himself as more than able to meet every need we could ever have. As exciting as that is, understand that characteristic is part of the 'image and likeness' of His that we carry. Because of Him, we've been designed to be more than equipped to meet every need we'll encounter. God isn't intimidated by our adopting a 'more than enough' attitude. When you really think about it, you notice that's how He's fashioned us. You've never reached the limit of your brain's capacity. The time in the gym may have shown you the maximum number of weights you *have* lifted, but it didn't tell you (given the proper situation) the amount of weight you're *capable* of lifting. What are the limits to your potential? Chances are, you don't know because you've not yet reached it. I like to consider our true potential as limitless. Not to say that it doesn't have a limit, but what difference does a limit make if we are never able to find it? As expansive as the universe is, God has designed us in the same fashion.

We have never reached the end of our provisions. We may have reached the end where we were looking, but

that's it. You've never run out of money. You've only
ran out of money in *your pocket*. You've never run out
of food. You've only run out of food in *your
refrigerator*. You've never run out of support. You've
only run out of support in *that group of people*. We don't
run out of things. We only run out of things *where we
are looking*. Change where you're looking, and you'll
change what you find. It sounds like a word game, but
trust that it isn't. There's an endless supply to everything
we need. If there weren't, no one would have any. If
there were no happiness, no one would have any. If there
were no love, no one would feel any. If there were no
peace, no one would have any. If anyone has it,
everyone may have it, but we may have to change where
we search for it. There can be no end to our supply if
there is no end to our God.

Brian Anderson-Payne

6

The Clean-Up Crew

Surely goodness and mercy shall follow me all the days of my life, and I shall dwell in the house of the Lord my whole life long.
Psalm 23:6

Some things are worth being convinced of. Some things are worth *knowing*, not just *believing*. When you *know* something, your body reacts according. The sound in your voice is different when you *know* you have the right answer. The stride in your walk changes when you *know* you have the solution. You sit down with a knowing that the chair will hold you, and not just a strong belief. You exhale with a *knowing* that your next breath of air will be there to meet you. If you stopped at just the belief, we would be able to tell it. The confidence level is different for the person who holds a 'strong belief' that his chair will hold him, versus the one whose strong belief has matured to *knowing* it will hold him.

Indeed, a belief is where it begins. However, after putting that belief to the test, we typically mature to knowing. It's no longer just a belief. The theory has been tested and tried. It has been forged by being dipped in the flames of scrutiny.

Carl Jung, one of the fathers of modern psychology,

defines the difference between believing and knowing this way. *Beliefs most often depend on what other people say, think, claim and have learned from others. Beliefs are intellectual rather than heart centered; often conceptual rather than visceral. Knowing, on the other hand, results from our own direct and personal experience in life. It generally aligns with an inner yardstick or compass and is far more dependable and consequential.*

Read more:
http://www.patheos.com/blogs/notbornyesterday/2013/06/the-difference-between-believing-and-knowing/#ixzz3R50ugdb1

Read more:
http://www.patheos.com/blogs/notbornyesterday/2013/06/the-difference-between-believing-and-knowing/#ixzz3R50mHx1f

Restating Carl Jung in my own words, "We believe what others tell us. We know what we've personally experienced!" That begins to clarify why David used the word *surely*. He did not doubt that God would be good to him. And there was good reason for David to have this confidence. When had God ever *not* been good to him?

Now ask yourself that question. Many people walk around with a terrifying view of God as if He's some frightening character in the sky, searching for the opportunity to punish us. Question the things others told you about God and look at the one true God you've seen your whole life. Listen to the things He says about you. His desires for you are for good. They are not evil. His plans for you include abundance and overflow, not scarcity and lack.

Perhaps too much of our present-day theology was formed by people who met God under a completely different set of circumstances than we did.

Goodness and mercy certainly are a strange couple to keep *behind* you. Wouldn't you want those two out front, touching situations before you do? Here's the reason I'm thankful that goodness and mercy follow me, like David. Remember goodness is simply that. It's good action. Goodness is 'excellence of quality; the state of being good.' Mercy is compassion or forgiveness. Mercy is *not getting the penalty deserved.* With that definition, I don't mind having them *behind* me. We don't always make the best decisions or the healthiest choices. I'm a prime candidate ready to confess that I've not always received the penalty that certain crimes warranted. Have you ever ran outside in the dead of winter with no hat, coat or even proper shoes, only to come back inside and experience no effects of your foolishness? Have you ever done something that could have and, perhaps, should have produced a completely different, less favorable outcome, only to find that no such bad thing happened? Some would look at certain situations as a 'license to ill.' Not me. I see it as negative seeds that were planted but didn't have an opportunity to grow because goodness and mercy plucked them up and out in time.

When there's a consistent pattern of this, you come to expect it. I didn't say you take it for granted. When you take something for granted, you lack real appreciation for it. I am speaking of a pattern of thinking that comes with habitual experiences.

GOOD THINGS HAPPEN FOR ME!

In Daniel 3, three Hebrew boys had to stand before the angry king Nebuchadnezzar and give an answer as to why they'd continued to pray to God, though life-threatening laws had been placed forbidding them to do so. Their response to their accuser is astounding.

Daniel 3:15-18
(New Century Version, my emphasis):

"In a moment you will again hear the sound of the horns, flutes, lyres, zithers, harps, pipes, and all the other musical instruments. If you bow down and worship the statue I made, that will be good. But if you do not worship it, you will immediately be thrown into the blazing furnace. What god will be able to save you from my power then?"

Shadrach, Meshach, and Abednego answered the king, saying, "Nebuchadnezzar, we do not need to defend ourselves to you. If you throw us into the blazing furnace, the God we serve is able to save us from the furnace. <u>He will save us from your power, O king</u>. But even if God does not save us, we want you, O king, to know this: We will not serve your gods or worship the gold statue you have set up."

Clearly, these guys had a history of God looking out for them. A habitual way of thinking had been developed. God had always been there for them in the past, so there was no logical reason why they should expect less now.

When you're convinced of it, you cause & create it!

Some people are just convinced that their life is full of bad experience after bad experience. They've adopted the mindset, "If it ain't one thing, it's another!" And guess what? They're absolutely right! They experience problem after problem, hurdle after hurdle, setback after setback. But the weird thing is, they're not really experiencing setbacks. They're creating them. *We don't see the world as it is, we see it as we are.* — Anaïs Nin

If you expect to see bad things, I guarantee you that you will. The reverse works the same. If you're determined to see the good, that's what comes into focus. It's not that good or bad is happening any more or any less than it always has been, but it's what you've chosen to focus on. This is somewhat like the Baader Meinhof Phenomenon. You know how you purchase a car, and suddenly, *that* car appears everywhere? It really isn't, but you unconsciously keep an eye out for it and find it surprisingly often. I suggest you kick that same idea in gear as it relates to the goodness of God. If you'd make a list, you'd definitely find that you experience more good things than bad. Focus on that. Expect it. Create it.

SURELY THIS IS MY LIFE!

David had certainly had his share of problems and fearful situations, but he'd come to a conclusion concerning his predicament. There was no convincing him that he wouldn't have a great life. His sins or shortcomings didn't change that idea. No matter what problems he faced, he'd come to the conclusion that he would always recover. That expectation was fully met, for as Jesus told the centurion in Matthew 8:13, "Let it be just as you have believed."

THE POWER OF A DECISION

Sometimes, you just need to decide. Decide if you want to be happy or if you want to keep complaining. Basic as it sounds, a decision must be made. Decide if you want to make your marriage work or if you want to be single again. You've been given authority and dominion over your life. God is a gentleman who won't rob you of your power. However, He provides information to help us choose wisely. You don't have to search far for the answers either.

We have the mind of Christ (I Corinthians 2:16).

Choose to be happy. Choose to love and be loved. Choose to have good health. Choose to forgive those who've hurt you and to seek forgiveness of those you've hurt. Choose to maximize your full potential. Choose to see the good over the bad. Choose to leave the past in the past.

Choose to believe you can conquer anything because God is on your side. Choose life!

Chapter 1 Notes

Three *Take-Aways* found in this chapter

1)_____

_____

2)_____

_____

3)_____

_____

Three Ways To Apply

1)_____

_____

2)_____

_____

3)_____

_____

Chapter 2 Notes

Three *Take-Aways* found in this chapter

1)_____

_____

2)_____

_____

3)_____

_____

Three Ways To Apply

1)_____

_____

2)_____

_____

3)_____

_____

Chapter 3 Notes

Three *Take-Aways* found in this chapter

1)_____
_____

2)_____
_____

3)_____
_____

Three Ways To Apply

1)_____
_____

2)_____
_____

3)_____
_____

Chapter 4 Notes

Three *Take-Aways* found in this chapter

1)_____

_____

2)_____

_____

3)_____

_____

Three Ways To Apply

1)_____

_____

2)_____

_____

3)_____

_____

Chapter 5 Notes

Three *Take-Aways* found in this chapter

1)_____

_____

2)_____

_____

3)_____

_____

Three Ways To Apply

1)_____

_____

2)_____

_____

3)_____

_____

Chapter 6 Notes

Three *Take-Aways* found in this chapter

1)_____

_____

2)_____

_____

3)_____

_____

Three Ways To Apply

1)_____

_____

2)_____

_____

3)_____

_____

Call To Action!

It's not enough to simply have information. This book has handed you a great deal of that. The next step is implementation. The proverb says, 'When the student is ready, the teacher will appear'. It's time to show that you're 'ready' to move to the next level of your life. Look at situations differently. See problems as opportunities.

What tools have you had with you all along that you haven't used properly? What changes can you make in your life without changing your circumstances? Who's in your sphere of influence that can benefit from the new perspective you have? I encourage you not to wait for tomorrow, but begin making impact right now. You don't need 'things' to change. You need your mind to change. When you change your mind, you change your life.

Enjoy your road of discovery.

ABOUT THE AUTHOR

I could use this space to tell you about the books I've written, the music I've produced, the programs I've established or a myriad of other things I've done. However, I'll skip that opportunity. In a Phillipian scripture, Paul encourages us to *forget whats behind by focusing on what's ahead*. What is ahead is truly greater than what is behind. Therefore, all I need you to know about me is I'm passionate about positively *brainwashing* you to see things in a new light. Open your mind and heart to experience everything our incredible God created you to experience.

If this book empowers you to change for the better in any way, let that be what you consider concerning me.

God bless,

Brian Anderson-Payne

Website:www.brianandersonpayne.com
Email: info@brianandersonpayne.com